Survivors

In Search of a Voice

The Art of Courage

Barbra Amesbury

Woodlawn Arts Foundation

Woodlawn Arts Foundation

P.O. Box C655, Station Q

Toronto, Ontario

Canada, M4T 2N5

Woodlawn Arts Foundation is the private foundation of M. Joan Chalmers

Canadian Cataloguing in Publication Data

Amesbury, Barbra, 1948—

Survivors, in search of a voice : the art of courage.

Catalogue to accompany an exhibition held at the
Royal Ontario Museum, Toronto, Feb. 17-May 23, 1995 and
travelling to other venues.

ISBN 0-9699043-0-4

1. Cancer in art - Exhibitions. 2. Art, Modern -
20th century - Canada - Exhibitions. 3. Art, Canadian
- Exhibitions. 4. Breast - Cancer - Patients -
Canada - Biography. 5. Women artists - Canada -
Biography. I. Royal Ontario Museum. II. Woodlawn
Arts Foundation. III. title.

N8223.A64 1995   704.9'4961699449'07471   C95-930578-5

This book is dedicated to the generations of women

who died in silence — their stories untold.

IN THE BEGINNING.....

One morning in late November of '93 a large envelope appeared on my doorstep. Inside I found a catalogue from an art exhibition held at the National Museum of Women in Washington, D.C. The show was called *Breast Cancer Journal: Walking With The Ghosts Of My Grandmothers*. The artist, a breast cancer survivor, was Hollis Sigler. Using a unique combination of image and word, she had created a powerful testament to her battle with cancer. Glancing back at the envelope, I noticed a hastily scribbled message: Dear Barbra, Why don't we ever do things like this in Canada? — *Why indeed,* I thought.

Six months earlier, Joan Chalmers and I had decided we wanted to participate in the fight against breast cancer. We didn't have to be told there was a problem — our friends were dying. So we travelled to conferences, attended countless survivor gatherings, and even organized discussion groups. We listened and we learned. But the dilemma remained — *how* could we help. The arrival of that catalogue was quite fortuitous.

Rather than just one, we thought, why not commission a number of our country's best women visual artists to create works of art that would, somehow, give a "voice" to the thousands of women struggling with this disease. And since we couldn't assume that the artists would know anything about breast cancer, we would ask breast cancer survivors to "educate" the artists, to tell them what it was to be a woman living with cancer. Then, we mused, we would give the show to every major gallery and museum in Canada with the understanding that those institutions would allow all the cancer groups in that province to use the exhibition to raise money and awareness.

As the AIDS quilt was a moving symbol in the fight against that disease, so too, we felt, would this exhibition be a symbol. We envisioned that *Survivors, In Search of a Voice* would be seen by all as a monument to courage, and we hoped it would empower breast cancer survivors, their families, and their friends to lift the veil of silence that pervades this disease. Although it only took us a few hours to *dream* this project, it took us eighteen months of seven-day weeks to make it a reality.

Because one hundred breast cancer survivors had the courage to tell their stories, because twenty-four of our best artists created the finest work of their careers, and because hundreds of women and men gave us their support and expertise, the next time someone asks me: *Why don't we ever do things like this in Canada? —* I can say — *We did!*

Barbra Amesbury
Woodlawn Arts Foundation
January 1995

Nancy Edell

Artist

After talking with survivors and following the deaths of two friends from breast cancer,
I chose the "operation" as the central image for my hooked rug. In placing the operating table in a pool of water,
I make reference to the Greenpeace study identifying chlorine as a possible factor in this disease.
The warrior women in breast armour are Contemporary Art Nuns. They represent the courage of all those who
have undergone cancer treatment. And finally, I've portrayed visualization as a two-headed serpent.
Survivors use similar creatures to chase the cancer through the fluids and tissues of their bodies.

Nancy Edell is a multimedia artist living in Halifax, Nova Scotia.

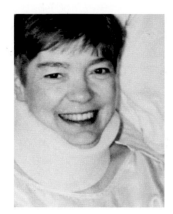

D I A N N E C R A I G

S u r v i v o r

My breast cancer metastasized to my bones. It was like fighting bush fires — I'd get one thing under control, and it would break through somewhere else. Around the middle of May, an X-ray of my neck revealed a deadly fracture. Suddenly I was playing Russian roulette. Is the cartridge going around? Is this the night I don't wake up? The neck could "snap" at any time, I was told, and it would be over — instantly. (Actually, I found the idea of a quick death comforting.)

The following Christmas I was still around. I was really quite surprised. You see, I'd planned everything. I'd made all the arrangements. Even my toenails were painted pink to match the dress I'll wear at my funeral. But because I'm still here, the polish has chipped. [Dianne's laughter fills the room.]

I'm fifty years old. I can't promise my family I'll reach the age of fifty-one. At least we've had the time to say good-bye, to say I'm sorry, and to say I love you. All in all, it's been a good summer.

Dianne Craig died on October 13, 1994.
The interview was conducted in the palliative care ward of a Regina hospital.

Jane Buckles

Artist

What you see before you is a woman "stopped dead" in her tracks. Behind her is strewn the once,
but no longer, important day timer, its pages crowded with the banalities of existence.
As with the metamorphosis a butterfly experiences, I see the survivor, through her cancer,
transformed into a beautiful creature with a heightened awareness and reverence to the
preciousness of life.

Jane Buckles is a multimedia artist who lives in Uxbridge, Ontario.

Barbara Cole

Artist

My original plan was to document the life and death struggle of a woman who had just been diagnosed
with breast cancer. But I was unable to find a subject who was willing to expose herself to that degree.
So, using a timer on my camera, makeup, and a bald cap I became my own model.
My mother is still in shock.

Barbara Cole is a photographer who lives in Toronto, Ontario.

12

ROSEMARY GADLER

Survivor

In 1989 I felt a small lump in my upper left breast. The gynecologist
told me it was nothing. "I wouldn't let anything bad happen to your
beautiful breasts," he vowed, dismissing my concerns. In '91 the same
breast became swollen and painful. The surgeon who examined me
said it looked malignant. An ultrasound and X-ray, reinforced with a
biopsy, not only confirmed his diagnosis, but indicated the cancer had
already spread to my lungs. In spite of a dismal prognosis — the disease
was classified as Stage 4 — I started chemotherapy. Miraculously, in

two short months, the lung metastasis vanished. (The removal of my breast was not recommended as it wouldn't increase my chances of survival.)

In June of '93 a pap smear betrayed the presence of cancerous cells. The results of a D and C were inconclusive to the type and origin. When I was twenty-four I watched, for two long and desperate years, as ovarian cancer killed my mother. *Anything but that,* I prayed. But God wasn't listening. Following a radical hysterectomy — they took the ovaries, fallopian tubes, and uterus — my worst fear was realized. "Am I going to die?" I asked, gripping the doctor's hand. "You've already lived longer than anyone thought you would," he replied, "and I expect you'll continue to surprise us."

Rosemary Gadler is thirty-six and lives in Montreal. In August of '94 tests found two lesions next to the sacroiliac, two on the membrane surrounding the liver, and a positive lymph node.

Barbara Todd
Artist

Initially, I wanted to make a piece that was celebratory. But the more I learned, the less likely that became.
I sensed that cancer was about business, power, and control. At the same time,
I was overwhelmed by the idea that in our society life and youth are embraced,
whereas old age and death are feared. My use of the coffin shape, combined with the spiral motif,
is an attempt to integrate the two.

Barbara Todd is a visual artist who lives in Montreal, Quebec.

15

Susan Low-Beer

Artist

As you approach my installation, the first section you encounter represents
the idea of a "whole" woman, someone who has yet to be diagnosed.

In the second phase of this piece the woman has lost a breast and her hair to cancer.
She is fighting for her life. And in the third, and final, sculpture she has faced her own mortality and survived.

Susan Low-Beer is a ceramist and sculptor who lives in Toronto, Ontario.

DOREEN JENKINS

Survivor

I had a radical mastectomy in 1967. When they were finished with me, all that remained was bone. One quarter of my body simply disappeared. To this day, my husband can't bear to look at me. At that time, because there was no such thing as chemotherapy, I was given cobalt treatments. I can remember lying on the table, terrified, my entire body covered with bags of sand for protection, and watching, transfixed, as the ominous pointed cone of that hideous machine spewed bolts of lethal radiation into my chest.

Six months later, my arm, due to the surgery, began to swell with fluid. It became so susceptible to infection that a cut or a burn would hospitalize me. Finding a way to elevate the arm for an extended period each day, allowing it to drain, was the only solution. Luckily, I had a creative friend in the iron and wire business. He invented a pulley system, an elaborate array of metal rods and cables that spanned the entire length of my bed. At one end he attached a weight for balance and on the other, directly over my pillow, a harness for the arm. I was a prisoner of that contraption every night — for eleven years.

Doreen Jenkins lives in Winnipeg. Even though she eventually lost a second breast to cancer, Doreen, now sixty-five, is still active in helping other women in her community cope with this disease.

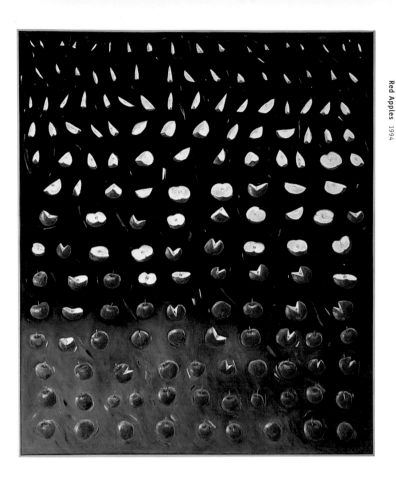

Red Apples 1994

Gathie Falk

Artist

To explain one of my paintings is, for me, to take a voyage into the unknown in a leaky boat with a blind navigator,
half an oar, and a bag over my head. Groping in the dark, I occasionally find markers that suggest
what my work may be about. In "Red Apples" I see not only the pain and horror of surgery but,
with survival, the redemptive beginnings of a new and richer life. If my markers are insufficient,
launch your own boat and look for more.

Gathie Falk is a painter who lives in Vancouver, British Columbia.

19

Jane Ash Poitras

Artist

In partnership with the women of Canada, I've created what I hope will be seen as both a monument to survivors and a memorial to those who have been killed by breast cancer. I encourage all those who have lost someone to this disease to write that person's name on the blackboard side of this installation. The hundreds of letters and photographs that were sent to me from cancer victims, their families, and their friends have been placed in an album that will travel with the show. Sitting on its own podium, the album is yours to read.

Jane Ash Poitras is a multimedia artist who lives in Edmonton, Alberta.

MARY DROVER

Survivor

I was assured the lump was nothing, but of course it was. I was thirty-four when I had my mastectomy. That was in 1984. A year later I had a recurrence — the cancer spread to my hip, my spine, and then to my knee. That's when I figured out I wasn't going to be okay. I started chemotherapy when the disease first appeared in my hip. By the time it lodged in my knee, I knew the drugs weren't working. Unfortunately, my oncologist agreed and I stopped all treatment. They told my family I had six months to live, but no one told me. That was ten years ago.

I'll be forty-five next week. I'm no longer a victim. I'm a survivor.

Cancer made me an activist. I was given my diagnosis in a crowded emergency room — then left in the dark. With surgery scheduled for the following week and absolutely no idea what my options were, I was expected to make what seemed to be life-and-death decisions. Look, I'm a smart person. Maybe not brilliant, but I can read a medical journal. I needed information, not condescension. I deserved better.

Mary Drover lives in Regina. She is a founding member of the Canadian Breast Cancer Network.

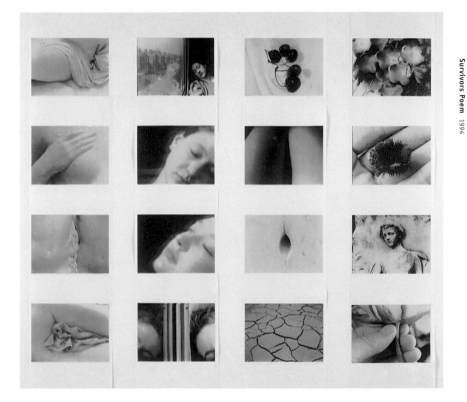

Wanda Koop
Artist

Because breast cancer is a big issue with a past, present, and future, I was convinced that whatever I did had to have a memorial quality about it. To match the magnitude of what I felt, I imprinted a series of video images on four large banners. In the first panel I talk of the separateness of mind and body, and in panel two, the reality of how alone we really are. Panel three, shot in Venice, is about life and desire, and the fourth panel is destiny. In its totality, I see this piece as our shared journey.

Wanda Koop is a multimedia artist living in Winnipeg, Manitoba.

23

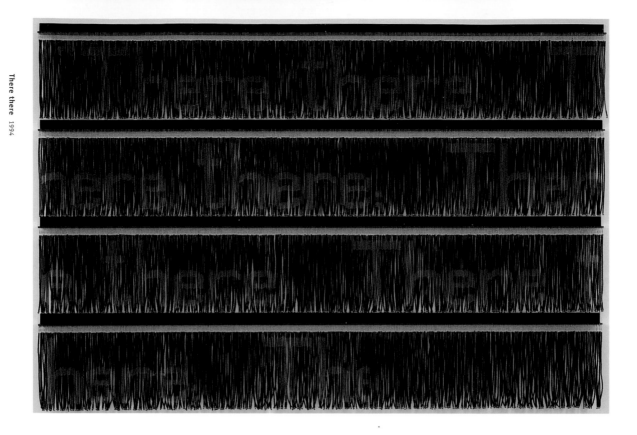

There there 1994

Colette Whiten
Artist

I felt that these women were being placated by their families, by their doctors — by the whole medical system: "There, there, there. It's going to be all right." And most of them feared that, unless they behaved themselves, unless they were good girls, they wouldn't get the treatment they needed. By using tiny coloured beads accumulated to look like a LED (light-emitting diode) display, I sought to introduce the notion that the technology available wasn't adequate to deal with this disease. We expect the medical profession to know, but they don't.

Colette Whiten is a multimedia artist living in Toronto, Ontario.

SHARON SOLOMON

Survivor

One night in bed I rolled over and felt something. It was a lump. Within days I was diagnosed with breast cancer. The surgeon removed the tumour, my nipple, and a large portion of lymph nodes. Then came chemotherapy and five weeks of radiation, so intense my skin turned black. I was in terrible shape. Eight months earlier, my periods had stopped. I thought, because of the treatments, I'd gone into early menopause. I was shocked when the doctor announced I was pregnant. There was no possibility of this baby being healthy, he said — all those drugs.

My gynecologist told me I had to have a "termination," but informed me, his voice edged with contempt, it was not a "procedure" he did. Over the next few weeks, I was denied treatment by at least five other physicians. Time was running out. I was about to enter my second trimester, and each day that passed put me more at risk. Finally, out of desperation, I called an abortion clinic — they saved my life.

I never told anyone this story. I was so ashamed. Wasn't my cancer enough?

Sharon Solomon is thirty-five and lives in Toronto.
She is currently involved in lobbying for daycare facilities
in all cancer hospitals.

Dawn MacNutt
Artist

My sculpture was woven on a loom from copper wire. After shaping it, I electroplated the piece,
a process where electrical current causes a chemical solution to plate and stiffen the work.

After each "bath," more chemicals and heat are applied to create the patina.

I was surprised by how similar the processing I used was to breast cancer treatment, and at the same time
shocked by the knowledge that radiation and chemotherapy are as indiscriminate in their
destructive potential as were my acids and chemicals.

Dawn MacNutt is a weaver and sculptor living in Halifax, Nova Scotia.

27

Susan Schelle
Artist

In this piece I'm dealing with the issues of identity and appearance and their impact on women in our society. When we met with the survivors, I was intrigued by how carefully they dressed — their hair, their makeup, the attention to detail. Even though they had lost one or both breasts and were in different stages of the disease, they all wanted to be seen as whole, as normal.

Susan Schelle is a mixed media artist who lives in Toronto, Ontario.

ALISON BAILES

Survivor

If breast cancer didn't actually cause the break-up of my second marriage, it certainly was the last straw. To give him his due, at least he stayed for the surgery and half my chemo. I was fighting for my life. He wasn't.

Sixteen months later, just after I got back from the National Breast Cancer Forum in Montreal, a bone scan uncovered metastases in my spine. The twelfth thoracic vertebra was all but destroyed. There was virtually nothing left surrounding the spinal cord. In less than three minutes, the oncologist gave me the bad news with a terse recommendation for palliative radiation. I'm a nurse. When someone says "palliative," I hear "end of the road." I've known that doctor for years. But when I reached out to her, across the desk, she recoiled in fear. "It's not catching," I said, slamming the door behind me.

I endured the radiation. For weeks, I couldn't sit, stand, or walk. The pain was so bad, I lived on Tylenol. But I survived. I didn't raise my kids all those years to make them orphans.

Alison Bailes is forty-four and lives in Winnipeg. She encourages women to be advocates for their rights. The quality of your treatment, she states, is not negotiable.

Margot Fagan

Artist

My work was inspired by a story one of the survivors told us. It seems that
the surgeon, a woman, who performed her mastectomy, grew up in a Mennonite
community. As a young girl, she had learned to make quilts.
As a result, the survivor explained, the scar on her chest, due to this doctor's
expert stitchery, was a work of art.

Margot Fagan is a textile artist who lives in Toronto, Ontario.

31

Mary Pratt

Artist

Using two packages of super-active yeast, I made bread dough and placed it in a clear glass bowl.

As the breast-like mound began to rise, its cells, like cancer cells, started to multiply at an ever-increasing rate. Suddenly, it was out of control. No matter how many times I punched it down, the dough — the cancer — kept growing. The photographs I took were quite ominous, and I think I've captured that in my painting.

Mary Pratt is a painter who lives in Newfoundland.

32

MARIE DUEN

Survivor

In 1988, the year following my breast cancer surgery, I participated in a New Age therapy seminar in New York. During a workshop exercise in which I was chosen to relate my dreams to the group, Jean, the instructor, called upon me to talk of my cancer. Suddenly, without warning, a damn inside me burst and I was swept up in an uncontrollable torrent of seething emotion. Blinded by tears, I described in minute detail how, from the age of seven, I had been sexually abused by my two older brothers. "Do you believe," Jean probed, "that the denial and repression of those sordid acts, for all these years, caused your cancer?" "Yes," I replied, in my first act of healing, "I do."

Marie Duen is forty-one and lives in Vancouver. When asked,
half of the 150 people in Marie's New York therapy group admitted to having
been abused as children. Of those, a significant percentage of the
women had experienced cancer.

Irene F. Whittome
Artist

For me the egg symbolizes the fragility of life and the inevitability of death. By creating a hole in each
egg, I prepared them for ovulation, and the birth and rebirth that follows.
Even though I'm not comfortable being the translator of others' emotions, the truth was painfully apparent.
On the issue of breast cancer, we're all partners in the art of surviving.

Irene F. Whittome is a multimedia artist who lives in Montreal, Quebec.

Aganetha Dyck
Artist

Hive Bodice is about cells, fragile cells containing sensuous, mysterious substances. Cells that are shaped, reshaped, filled, drained, cleansed, painted, prodded, invaded, and monitored.
Powerful and sexual, they are filled with nurture and desire.
Mutant and diseased, they brim with death.

Aganetha Dyck is a multimedia artist living in Winnipeg, Manitoba. This piece was done in collaboration with the honeybees.

CETT DI FALCO-ANTONACCI

Survivor

I was twenty-three when a biopsy uncovered a cancerous tumour hiding behind a fibroid. I was given a lumpectomy and radiation. Eighteen months later, shortly after my marriage, I had a recurrence. They performed another lumpectomy. Only this time, because so many lymph nodes were positive, the oncologist prescribed eight months of aggressive chemo. It was pure hell. Immune to the radiation that followed, the cancer metastasized to my chest wall. There's nothing else we can do, they said, just go home and try to live each day to its fullest. I was twenty-six years old — I wasn't ready to die.

My whole family went to war. My dad did the research, my mom took care of the house, and my husband took care of me. As the cancer moved into my lungs, a tumour the size of a plum broke through the skin above my breast. I was hysterical. In August of '94 I convinced my family to go with me to Quebec City. I took them to the church of Saint Anne de Beaupré. It was so beautiful, so peaceful. Even though my father was still angry with God for all that had happened, we prayed. That night, back at the hotel, the tumour exploded — then disappeared. I took it as a sign.

Cett DiFalco-Antonacci died in Toronto on December 27, 1994,
at the age of twenty-eight.

Screen 1994

Christine Davis
Artist

Faced with the reality of cancer and my own fears, I began thinking about how the physical body
moves through loss to become, refocused by tenacity and will, another body —
the same, yet different. I wanted my work to be both haunting and full of hope.
The emphasis not on a final physical state, but on the process of discovery.

Christine Davis is a multimedia artist who lives in Toronto.

Renée Van Halm

Artist

I was surprised by the number of young women who are survivors.

I had always assumed that breast cancer was a disease of old women — women long past their child-bearing years whose beauty was no longer "marketable" in society.

I was concerned that — whatever I did — it would honour, not belittle or sensationalize, their lives.

I wanted to speak for them as well as to them. The premise of my piece is quite simple.

One in nine women are going to get breast cancer. The only question is who?

Renée Van Halm is a multimedia artist who lives in Vancouver, British Columbia.

EVA BERETI

Survivor

I lost all faith in my doctors and their medicine because of the racist treatment I received when I got cancer. Still weak from a mastectomy but no longer willing to tolerate the constant degradation, I dragged myself from a hospital bed and went home. For weeks, burning sweet grass every day, I tried to cleanse my mind and regain my strength. I was caught between two worlds. Staking my life on the old ways, I returned to my people, to the sweat lodge.

I shared a pipe with the medicine man and told him I had cancer. He listened, said very little, then beckoned me into the lodge. Inside, joined by other members of the tribe, we sat in a circle around a pile of glowing rocks. The air, thick with heat, crackled. Summoned from a dream state, I was instructed to lie down in front of the holy elder and with the wings of an eagle he took the cancer from my body.

Eva Bereti is fifty-six and lives in Edmonton.
Jane Ash Poitras calls Eva a shamaness,
a woman of mystical powers.

Annette Francoise

Artist

I blew two quilts before I did this one. The burden of responsibility was crushing.
I tried using quotations and poetry, but it wasn't me. I'm an abstract visualist.
The work I created represents the physical and emotional sides of cancer.
The centre of the piece, like the disease, is quite chaotic and full of jagged shapes.
The outside, the frame, is order and how things should be.

Annette Francoise is a textile artist who lives in Dundas, Ontario.

43

Interior

Barbara Klunder

Artist

My first impression of the survivors I met was that, in spite of breast cancer,
they were all courageous and brimming with personal insight.
Then, after a year of soaking up information and statistics, my anger emerged. I realized that our governments and the
powerful elite of our society were practicing the politics of avoidance. What if we all considered
cancer an enemy and killer equal to fascism and dedicated ourselves, re-designed society, for a WAR to find
solutions. It's not impossible. P.S. Open the box.

Barbara Klunder is a multimedia artist who began this project in Vancouver,
British Columbia, but has since moved back to Toronto, Ontario.

CATHERINE BLACK

Survivor

The day I turned fifty, I decided it was time for a complete checkup. I'd read about the Ontario Breast Screening Program in the newspaper; it seemed like a good place to start. The mammography came back with a "red flag." Even though I felt no lump, something was there. The surgeon gave me all the possible scenarios, then recommended a mastectomy. The choice was mine.

Frustrated by ignorance, I asked my sister and a friend, both of whom worked in the medical establishment, to send me every word that existed on the subject of breast cancer. It was only then that I was able to make an informed decision. I had a mastectomy, and have never regretted it.

The day they removed the bandages was the worst. Flat on one side with no breast, I was half male. And then I thought: It really is cancer. But gradually, one day at a time, I healed. I faced my own mortality and survived. If it comes back, I'll fight it. I still want to be here.

Catherine Black is a volunteer with the Ontario Breast Screening Program.
Her primary focus is ethnic and community outreach.

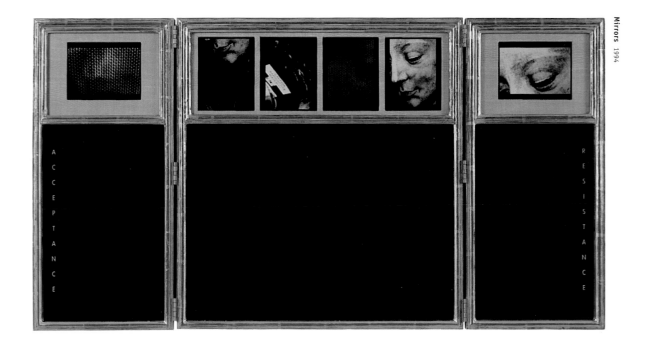

Barbara Steinman

Artist

To express what was true for me in this project, I chose to use the mirror, an artifact of truth and denial.
Each woman finds within herself what she has the strength and courage to resist and what she must
somehow accept. These are not fixed choices.
The images are rephotographed studies for the conservation of a marble Madonna.
Her demeanor, as damage to her neck is scrutinized through an enormous X-ray lens,
looked the way I feel when I submit to any invasive medical treatment.

Barbara Steinman is a multimedia artist living in Montreal, Quebec.

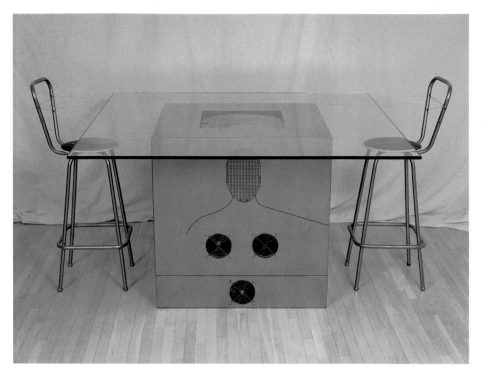

Donna Kriekle
Artist

My piece takes the form of a table. On the issue of breast cancer, it is a table of contents.
As we gather around this cancerous table of *chance*, each of us becomes a player, either as a spectator or as a participant.
What are the odds?

Donna Kriekle is a multimedia artist who lives in Regina, Saskatchewan.

MAGGIE MUTO

Survivor

My family doctor said it was a fibroid adenoma. He told me it was benign and the only reason to have it removed would be cosmetic. I trusted him. Months later, when I could still feel the lump, I voiced my concern. It's really nothing, my doctor assured, don't worry about it. But I did. Careful not to offend him, I pleaded with the doctor to send me to a surgeon. Still insisting it was a waste of time, he grudgingly relented. The biopsy came back positive. I had adenoma carcinoma — cancer.

During my lumpectomy, they discovered that seven out of the ten lymph nodes were involved. The doctors believed I was going to die, so I was placed at the bottom of the list for treatment. If it hadn't been for my friend Susan, I wouldn't be here today. She harassed everybody. Once she even took the diamond ring off her finger and, shoving it in some doctor's hand, yelled: "Get her radiation, now!" Along with six horrible months of chemotherapy, I got my radiation.

Maggie Muto is forty-three and lives in Mississauga, Ontario.
Some days are still a struggle, she says.

Sylvie Bélanger

Artist

After listening to the breast cancer survivors' testimonies,
I was haunted by the words: sensuality, voluptuousness, desire,
breast, fragmentation, feel, fear, hope, share, tell, life, and death.
In this work I am investigating the margins between the
"absence" and the "presence" of the body, as it is torn
between technology and emotions.

Sylvie Bélanger is a multimedia artist living in Toronto, Ontario.

Biberon Robert 1994

Spring Hurlbut

Artist

The two oval biberons (nursing bottles) were made in France in the 1860's.
It was felt that, because of their design, they would be more appealing to
the infant. Symbolizing the breast, the biberon functions in its absence.
Substitution and absence are conditions which continue to face women,
their bodies, and their identities.

Spring Hurlbut is a multimedia artist living in Toronto, Ontario.

MONICA WILSON

Survivor

At the age of fifty-five I was diagnosed with breast cancer. My husband had just left me and I was still reeling from my daughter's suicide. I wanted to die. Life was far too painful and cancer was the easy way out.

Cerebellar sarcoma struck my son when he was only seven years old. The experts concluded that death, within months, was a certainty. At fourteen, still alive, the cancer metastasized to his spine and at nineteen, confined to a wheelchair, he had a recurrence. That stubborn little bugger turned forty-one this year. He never gave up. How could I?

Monica Wilson is sixty-nine and lives in Edmonton. She believes that surviving cancer empowered her to create a new and better life.

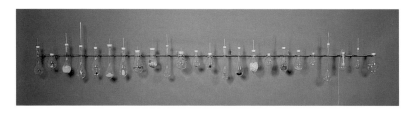

Catherine Widgery
Artist

In my work I try to render visible not just the horror of breast cancer
but the complex range of emotions survivors experience. Infected with cancer,
these women's breasts are suddenly perceived by society in a different light.
Femininity itself is challenged. What had been sexual and maternal symbols are suddenly
clinical specimens, their sensuality forsaken. As much as anything, this work is about
the isolation each woman feels when confronted with her own mortality.

Catherine Widgery is a sculptor and multimedia
artist who lives in Montreal, Quebec.

MACK KOHOUT FOR JOANNE KOHOUT

Survivor

It was May of '93 and we had just retired when Joanne found the lump. We travelled to Halifax for a needle biopsy. Three days after it came back positive, Joanne had a lumpectomy. The chemotherapy that followed was a disaster. Reacting badly to the drugs, her white cell count dropped off the charts. In stark contrast, the radiation was a breeze. After weeks of uncertainty, the surgeon, armed with the results of a baseline test, pronounced Joanne "clean." "You'll never have cancer again," he said. We were on top of the world. With our bags packed and the camper gassed, we set out to see Canada.

Months later, we were sitting in the mountains of British Columbia sipping champagne when Joanne's lower back and shoulder began to ache. Sensing trouble, we turned east and headed for home. Outside of Calgary, Joanne appeared breathless and complained of fatigue. *I put my foot to the floor.* Stopping in London, Ontario, I checked Joanne into a hospital. An X-ray detected the buildup of fluid in and around one of her lungs. Given her history, the doctor concluded that Joanne's cancer was back. By the time we got to Halifax, her breathing was laboured and she was in constant pain. Tests revealed the disease had spread to her chest wall and lymph nodes. As if that wasn't enough, small tumours were breaking through the skin and a bone marrow tap brought more bad news. The bloody cancer had spread to every inch of her body.

Grasping at straws, Joanne gained access to a new drug called 7-14-X. But the two doctors who had promised to administer it changed their minds at the last moment. Even though we eventually found a doctor who agreed to help, it was too little, too late. We just ran out of time.

On our last night together, Joanne sat huddled in a chair as I knelt on the floor in front of her. She folded her arms around my neck, our foreheads touched, and our souls made love. The next morning Joanne died.

Joanne Kohout died on November 28, 1994, at the age of fifty-one, just days before her scheduled interview for this book. A resident of New Glasgow, Nova Scotia, Joanne's husband Mack told her story.

In the end....

I wish to thank M. Joan Chalmers O. C., O. Ont., my partner and mentor, for her absolute dedication to *Survivors*. Joan is, as was her late father, Floyd, regarded as one of Canada's premiere philanthropists. Her generosity and leadership were responsible for the success of this entire project. And I am indebted to Clarice Chalmers, Joan's sister-in-law. No stranger to the realities of cancer, Clarice made the production of this book possible. And finally, to the artists and survivors who came together to create the "art of courage"—Without you, *Survivors* would still be just a dream. Your *voices* were heard.

CREDITS

The beautiful art photography was done by Cheryl O'Brian and the stunning black and white portraits are by John Reeves (except for Dianne Craig and Joanne and Mack Kohout). The editor was Meg Taylor and the transcriptions were done by Susan Crammond. This book was designed with great sensitivity by Adams + Associates and printed by C.J. Graphics. The original logo for *Survivors* was designed by Mark Talbot-Kelly.

Also . . .

I wish to thank northAmerican Van Lines for their participation in this project as a tour sponsor, Nancy Hushion and her crew for tour management, and, in fear of leaving someone out, let me just say how grateful I am to everyone who helped make this show and this book a success.

SURVIVORS, IN SEARCH OF A VOICE:
THE ART OF COURAGE

Exhibition Itinerary

Royal Ontario Museum
Toronto, Ontario
February 17 – May 22, 1995

**The Gallery Stratford/
Stratford Festival**
Stratford, Ontario
June 9 – September 10, 1995

Art Gallery of Nova Scotia
Halifax, Nova Scotia
November 11, 1995 – January 1, 1996

MacKenzie Art Gallery
Regina, Saskatchewan
January 15 – February 25, 1996

Vancouver Art Gallery
Vancouver, British Columbia
March 20 – May 26, 1996

Winnipeg Art Gallery
Winnipeg, Manitoba
June 16 – August 25, 1996

Glenbow Museum
Calgary, Alberta
September 14 – December 7, 1996

*....it's your show. Let us know
where you want it.*

List of Works

Nancy Edell, *Page 8*
Operating 1994
Hooked rug (found wool
rag and burlap)
44" x 55½" x ¼"

Jane Buckles, *Page 11*
Annie 1994
Paper mache and mixed media
36" x 32" x 33"

Barbara Cole, *Page 12*
**[1]Constant Reminder [2]Public
Scrutiny [3]Body Betrayal** 1994
SX-70 iris prints
3 x (27" x 27")

Barbara Todd, *Page 15*
Overlay 1994
wool and cotton
87" x 68"

Susan Low-Beer, *Page 16*
Short Light, Long Dark 1994
Clay and steel
3 x (72" x 48" x 24")

Gathie Falk, *Page 19*
Red Apples 1994
Oil on canvas
78" x 60" x 2"

Jane Ash Poitras, *Page 20*
Courage Blanket 1994
Mixed media
66" x 66" x 5"

Wanda Koop, *Page 23*
Survivors Poem 1994
cotton-screen print
and wood frame
4 panels x (16' x 40")

Colette Whiten, *Page 24*
There there 1994
Glass beads suspended from
aluminum angle wall mount
52" x 75" x 1½"

Dawn MacNutt, *Page 27*
Transcendence 1994
Copper wire woven,
electroplated, and patinated
65" x 24" x 22"

Susan Schelle, *Page 28*
Calendar 1994
Porcelain plates, gold leaf,
and silk screen
12 x 8¼"

Margot Fagan, *Page 31*
Do You Know How it Feels? 1994
Pieced fabric with quilting and
embroidery (cotton and wool)
52" x 19" x 5"

Mary Pratt, *Page 32*
Bread Rising 1994
Canvas on stretchers
and gesso ground
36" x 48" x 1"

Irene F. Whittome, *Page 35*
**Femme Inconnue/
Unknown Woman** 1994
Ostrich eggs, mahogany
and birch wood, and glass
45¼" x 36¼" x 24"

Aganetha Dyck, *Page 36*
Hive Bodice 1994
Wooden hive, glass bodice,
beeswax , metal, and honey
17½" x 18¾" x 22"

Christine Davis, *Page 39*
Screen 1994
Silver print
82" x 56" x 2"

Renée Van Halm, *Page 40*
One In Nine 1994
Mirror, paint, and wooden disks
#1 (128" x 24" x 4½")
#2 (23" x 1½")

Annette Francoise, *Page 43*
July 7 1994
Linen, antique satin, silk, cotton,
wool, velvet, felt, corduroy, and
synthetic fabric — machined,
stitched, and quilted
70" x 76" x 2"

Barbara Klunder, *Page 44*
MonkeyBusinessMen 1994
Acrylic painting on wooden cabinet,
embroidery, paper, and collage
24" x 12" x 6"

Barbara Steinman, *Page 47*
Mirrors 1994
Etched mirrors, photographs,
and a hand-gilded frame
22" x 36" x 1¼"

Donna Kriekle, *Page 48*
**If I Were To Need
A Mastectomy . . .** 1994
Sony stereo TV, Sony VCR,
aluminum base, two chairs,
colour-copy transfer on acetate,
silver elastic thread, and glass
54" x 54" x 31"

Sylvie Bélanger, *Page 51*
Comme une ombre sur le corps 1994
Colour photographs, glass,
and optical lens
5 x (30" x 6" x 3")

Spring Hurlbut, *Page 52*
Biberon Robert 1994
Two glass biberons, silver wire, linen,
wood frame, and plexiglass
19" x 16¼" x 3½"

Catherine Widgery, *Page 54*
Don't Touch / Please Touch 1994
Blown glass, stainless steel,
and mixed media
15' x 2' x 1'